IMAGES OF ENGLAND

RUSHOLME AND VICTORIA PARK

Wilmslow Road, Rusholme

IMAGES OF ENGLAND

RUSHOLME AND VICTORIA PARK

JILL CRONIN AND FRANK RHODES

TEMPUS

Frontispiece: Looking north along Wilmslow Road, a shop-lined main road, in 1907. This was the turnpiked route from the city of Manchester out through Rusholme to Wilmslow, with a toll bar south of Moss Lane East (late Clock House Lane). On the left is the now demolished Rusholme Congregational church. On the right Dickenson Road leads off beyond the Birch Villa Hotel (now Hardy's Well).

First published 2006

Tempus Publishing Limited
The Mill, Brimscombe Port,
Stroud, Gloucestershire, GL5 2QG
www.tempus-publishing.com

© Jill Cronin and Frank Rhodes, 2006

The right of Jill Cronin and Frank Rhodes to be identified as the Authors of this work has been asserted in accordance with the Copyrights, Designs and Patents Act 1988.

British Library Cataloguing in Publication Data.
A catalogue record for this book is available from the British Library.

ISBN 0 7524 4198 1

Typesetting and origination by Tempus Publishing Limited.
Printed in Great Britain.

Contents

Acknowledgements

We should like to thank all those who have helped us and the people who have given kind permission for us to include their photographs:
Frank Blood, Mrs Pat Crompton, Susan Hyde Fielding, Mr G.H. Harrop, John Hynes, Robert Hynes, Bernard Lackey, Dr Chris Lee at www.itsahotun.com (Film Studios (M/C) Ltd), Colin and Rosemary Morton of the Methodist International Home, Gay Oliver, Dr Timothy Stibbs and Peter Helm of the Rusholme and Fallowfield Civic Society, Victor Sayer, Sandra Tomlinson, Graham Walters, Alan Ward and the Principal and staff at Xaverian College.

Dedicated to Peter Helm in appreciation of his knowledge of Rusholme.

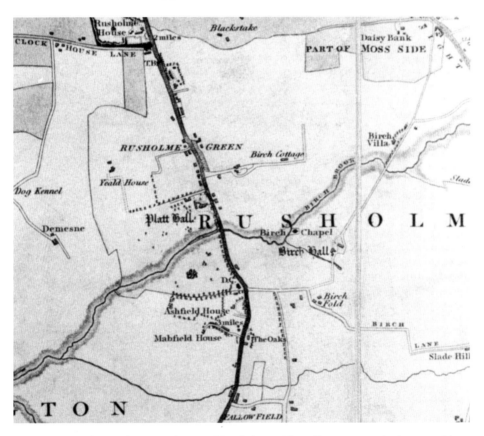

Johnson's map of 1820, showing a then rural Rusholme, with a village green and criss-crossed by brooks. Soon suburbia arrived, with increased roads and housing, the enclave of Victoria Park and three parks created from estates once centred on large halls. Rusholme is bounded by Moss Side on the west, Fallowfield to the south, Levenshulme and Longsight to the east, plus a detached part of Moss Side and Gorton and Chorlton-on-Medlock to the north.

Introduction

Rusholme was once a village in the vast parish of Manchester, within the Salford Hundred and the sub-Manor of Withington, itself within the Manor of Manchester. Its name is Anglo-Saxon, deriving from 'rush' or 'reed' with 'holme' meaning flat, low-lying land by a river or stream. *Russum* is recorded as early as 1235, being spelt variously *Risshulm*, *Rysshulme* and *Ryssheholm* until it stabilised as *Rushulme* in 1649. The name describes its features: once mossland with reedy pools (*laches*) on clay subsoil. No river or canal ever passed through Rusholme but the Gore Brook does, known variously as the Rush, Birch or Platt Brook. South of the village, where Fallowfield now lies, was the forest of Arden or Hardy.

The boundaries of Rusholme are quite complicated. To the north lies Chorton-on-Medlock, with Whitworth Park straddling this border. To the west is Moss Side, with a small detached area of Moss Side within Rusholme near Daisy Bank Road. To the south lies Fallowfield with Platt Fields Park crossing this border. To the east lies Longsight and Laversholme. Birch-in-Rusholme lay across Rusholme and Longsight. For this book we have followed the boundary denoted by William Royle in 1914.

The population growth reflects Rusholme's development from village into township and later suburb of the city of Manchester. In 1655 there were 14 ratepayers, by 1714, 40 families of 200 people, in 1801, 726 people rising to 1,708 by 1831, 3,679 in 1851 and 20,000 by 1914. The village was centred on Rusholme Green, bordered on its west by Wilmslow Road and stretching between Lloyd Street and Dickenson Road.

Eight Roman coins were discovered in the Gore Brook near Anson golf course in the 1890s and Anglo-Saxon Nico Ditch crosses through the township. The village was centred around the halls and estates of Platt, Birch and Slade. Farming and handloom weaving were the main occupations, with housing concentrated along the main roads, with scattered farms. Manchester centre provided the market and Birch probably had its own corn mill on the brook. Turf was cut from the mossland for fuel. These cottage industries continued into the early eighteenth century.

During the 1800s the gradual change began from a village into a suburban, residential area. In 1837 Rusholme township became part of the Chorlton Poor Law Union. Merchants, some manufacturers, shopkeepers and gentlefolk moved into the area, including Moroccan merchants in their distinctive clothing. The unsuccessful Brighton Grove housing scheme was set up in 1834. In 1837 a private company began the select housing estate named Victoria Park, which was to cover about a fifth of Rusholme, attracting merchants of many nationalities, especially German. As a Turnpike road with toll gates, between the city of Manchester and Wilmslow, Wilmslow Road attracted trade and shops along its route, as well as the gentry moving out of the city.

In 1849 Rusholme Local Board of Health was formed, which organised public services. This was a far cry from the four private watchmen and one policeman of village days. By 1854 there were two public houses and sixteen beer houses in the township. In the 1870s a housing boom provided both professional and working class housing off Wilmslow Road, as people moved out of the city and more jobs were available locally. In 1885 Rusholme became part of the city of Manchester, in spite of strong opposition from Rusholmites. The result was well-lit and well-kept roads, public parks and a public library. The three parks were established from the estates at Birch and Platt Halls and Grove House (Whitworth Park).

Religion has been prominent in Rusholme with its chapels and churches influencing people across Manchester. The first, early Birch chapel attracted dissenting priests and congregation, which resulted in Platt Unitarian chapel being opened on Wilmslow Road and Holy Trinity and St James's Anglican churches being founded in the 1840s.

Post-war, Rusholme has changed in two ways. The University of Manchester has expanded along Wilmslow Road and into Victoria Park, taking over many of the large houses and introducing a student population, as has Xaverian College. Manchester Grammar School and Manchester High School for Girls have both moved out to Rusholme. During the 1960s and 1970s immigration has brought many Asian and West Indian people into the area and Wilmslow Road has become cosmopolitan, with many ethnic shops and restaurants often dubbed 'Curry Mile'.

This book attempts, using over two hundred photographs, to show the importance of and chart the changes in Wilmslow Road; the people living in Rusholme who have influenced Manchester life; the growth and decline of Victoria Park; the halls and estates transformed into public parks; life at church and at school and the varied entertainment offered in the town. Leslie's Pavilion and the Rusholme Theatre provided shows, the Casino and Trocadero cinema and the former Methodist chapel on Dickenson Road was home to Film Studios (Manchester) Ltd and then to the BBC television service. Stars like Frank Randle, Robert Donat and Tessie O'Shea worked in Rusholme.

The history of Rusholme belongs to everyone in Manchester, as the town has affected the rest of the city with its parks, institutions, entertainment and influential residents. It has been home to foreign incomers ever since the start of Victoria Park. This book will be of interest to all were born and bred in Rusholme, to students who now live and study here and to newcomers who have made Rusholme their home.

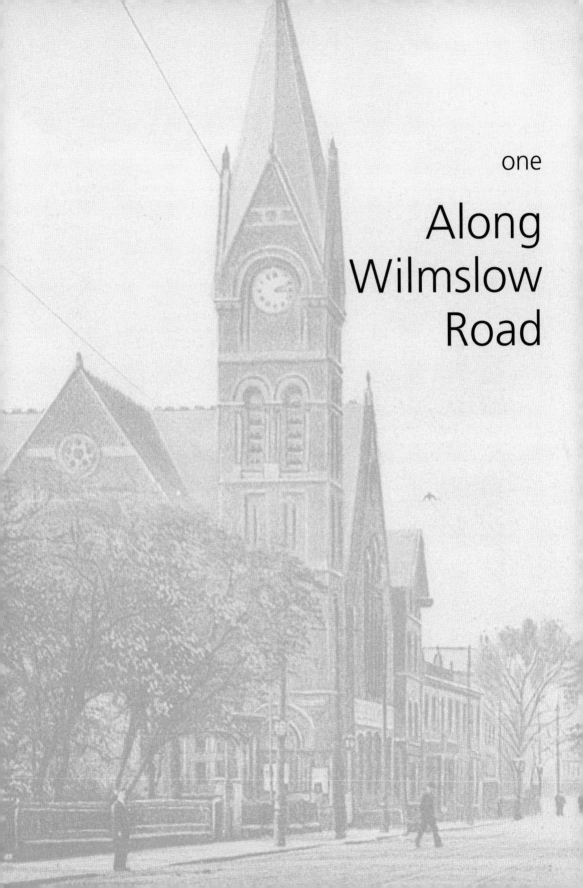

one

Along Wilmslow Road

Looking northwards along Wilmslow Road in 1906. On the left (west side) the tall premises of Walter Carter's furniture depository dominate the scene, separated from the Manchester Carriage Co. by Little Western Street. Next comes Great Western Street with Samuel Moseley's laundry in the foreground. Originally named the Manchester Carriage & Tramways Co. it operated horse trams with over seven hundred horses. Later it ran hansom cabs and private hire with a riding school. The Rusholme Electric cinema, followed by the Rusholme repertory theatre, later used the site (see page 117). The east side of the road is still lined with this tall row of shops.

Opposite above: Billhead of the firm of Walter Carter's storage depository on Wilmslow Road, in 1933. He became the Manchester agent for Harrods of London, as well as for the Manchester department store Kendal Milne & Co. The depository was built in 1876 on the site of the old toll bar and the Manchester Carriage Co. next door was on the site of a row of thatched cottages, which included two almshouses for Rusholme's poor.

Opposite below: An early 1930s advertisement for a motor van built by the firm of S.H. Bond. Samuel Harold Bond was a coachbuilder on Little Western Street just off Wilmslow Road. The firm moved to the new Sharston industrial estate at Wythenshawe in around 1952 and finally closed in 1969. This art deco van, built for Thomas Kerfoot's of Bardsley Bridge, advertises their Vapex tablets. Bond's also produced 'Monty's Caravan', a mobile command caravan for General Montgomery in the 1940s.

City Office : KENDAL MILNE & CO.,

DEANSGATE, MANCHESTER,

Dec 22nd 1933

M R R Smethurst   21 Arrung Gardens
                                    Manchester

To WALTER CARTER,
(HARRODS. LTD.)
THE DEPOSITORIES, RUSHOLME, MANCHESTER.

S 8
5610

1933

To Storage of Furniture from Oct. 33
      to Dec 31 33.   12 weeks   4/-   28 .
                                            ok

Dec 16   " delivering carpets in advance
          to Flat. 6. Abbey Lawn
          Seymour Grove . Old Trafford
          altering & fitting , supplying railway
          runners for curtains & fitting sundry
          items at house   8 .

      21   " delivering all goods except bedstead
          to the above address   3
                                             ₤ 10 .
                                          ₤ 14 18

Banff Terrace on Wilmslow Road, *c.* 1910. Built in the grounds of Banff House, once home to Sydney Mason JP, it lay on the east side of the road, opposite Moss House and south of Rusholme Place. On the right is No. 3, Frederick Burchill's jewellery shop with trunks piled up outside. Next at No.2 is the Park Circulating library, which was also the Public Telephone & Cable office, plus an agent for Pullar's of Perth and sold fancy goods and stationery. Outside, the placards advertise the papers *Pall Mall*, *Forget-me-Not* and the *London Opinion*. At No. 1 is a food shop, with a woman peering out. Later it was occupied in turn by a milliner, house furnisher and wardrobe dealer.

Opposite above: The east side of Wilmslow Road, opposite Carter's Depository, in the 1910s. Trams mingle with horses, carts and delivery bikes. First on the right is a café and Clifton's confectioner's shop selling fine chocolate. Next are Bratt & Hobson's 'the Tea Men', which by 1920 was a dairy, then Holden's photographer's shop and next was a branch of the Manchester & Salford Savings Bank. Banff Terrace lay north of the row.

Rusholme Tram Stage, Manchester.

WILMSLOW R^D RUSHOLME

Looking north along Wilmslow Road in the 1920s. Tall buildings lie opposite the Manchester Carriage Co. On the right are a milliner's and furrier's shops, next to The Target, children outfitter's and fancy drapery. Then comes Albert Inman, tobacconist, followed by William Timpson bootmaker, a linen shop, hairdresser's and then a sub-post office (in 1901 a stationer's). Right of the milliner's shop is a tailor's on the corner of Dagenham Road.

The name plaque on the north corner of Loyd (now Walmer) Street, with the initials W.S. and dated 1848. Loyd/Lloyd Street turns off Wilmslow Road on its east side. W.S. Lloyd built the houses near the bottom end, occupying one himself. The shop on the corner here was a butcher's for many years.

Frank and Fred Blood stand outside their antique shop in 1961. The shop once stood between Lloyd and Thurloe Streets on the east side of Wilmslow Road. From the early 1900s until the 1930s it was a fruiterer's shop. James Frederick Blood, an expert in porcelain, started in Knott Mill and settled here in 1945. His sons closed the business down in 1965 after his death. Fred ran evening classes and Frank was expert at repairs and upholstery.

Looking north along Wilmslow Road, *c.* 1910. On the right are the shops of a draper (later a milliner), fruiterer, tailor, boot dealer and butcher, ending at Lloyd Street. On the left lies Walmer Street.

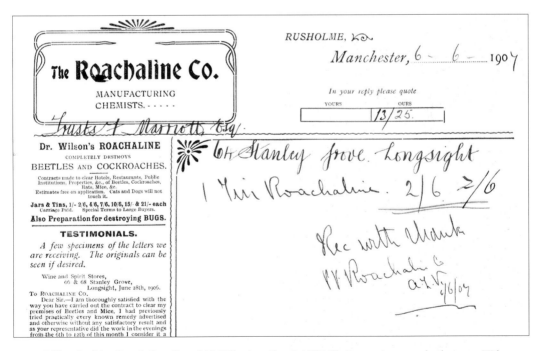

Billhead of the Roachaline Co. of 60, Wilmslow Road, 1907. Their premises once lay between Walmer and Grange Streets on the west side of the main road. As manufacturing chemists they specialised in Dr Wilson's Roachaline for destroying pests. The billhead contains recommendations from clients including hoteliers at Blackpool and Bristol. By 1945 they described themselves as 'vermin destroyers'.

Wilmslow Road, Rusholme

Above: Looking north along Wilmslow Road in the early 1900s. On the left lies Walmer Street and beyond the tall building of Walter Crane's depository. Right lies Thurloe Street with the Rusholme Bakery and Flour Stores on its corner, a bakery back in 1901 but by 1945 a Burgon's grocery store. Next come a private house, Benton's tobacconists shop and a bootmakers which later became a drapery. Beyond the two-storey, taller building was a branch of Seymour Mead & Co., the grocery chain.

Left: This building was a branch of the grocery chain of Seymour Mead & Co. from around 1901 until the late 1930s. It lies between Lloyd and Thurloe Streets. In 1945 it became a pressed tool manufacturers and then by 1965 it was the Rusholme Light Car Co.'s premises. The building is now an Indian restaurant.

Above: A row of thirteen shops forming Crescent Gate on Wilmslow Road, dated 1906. It was so-called because it lies near an entrance to Victoria Park at Crescent Range and Park Crescent. The row included, in the 1920s, the British and Argentine Meat Co. and a branch of Deacon's bank. In the 1940s it contained a branch of Dewhurst the butchers, a photographer and the bank just at the entrance to Victoria Park.

Right: The billhead of J.S. Breese, pharmaceutical chemists at 191 Wilmslow Road, in 1932. John Soley Breese established his chemists shop in 1840. Lying on the east side of Wilmslow Road, near to Rusholme Grove, it was sandwiched between a sub-post office and a fishmonger's shop. This bill came to £1 4s 1d for fifteen items over a period of three months, including Izal toilet rolls, Lux soap, Tidman's salt and Gillette razor blades.

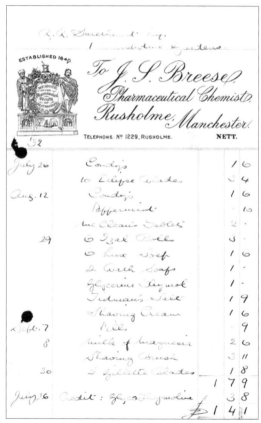

Above: This building housed the Manchester Corporation Electric Light and Traction works, which powered the trams along Wilmslow Road. On the left is Claremont Road (originally Granny Lane and later Monmouth Street). Today it houses the Indian Cottage restaurant. The row continues to Grandale Road with shops and a Temperance billiard hall upstairs.

Left: A coat of arms of the city of Manchester on the Electric Light and Traction works. Above are the letters MCEW for Manchester City Electricity Works, who built it to provide extra electricity for the trams. The building still stands on the west side of Wilmslow Road, opposite an entrance to Victoria Park. Eventually there was a substation there for the North West electricity board. The first purely electrical exhibition for Manchester was held on Platt Fields in 1908.

Above: Upstairs, over shops, these buildings housed the Temperance Billiard Halls Co., established in 1906. The hall was the flagship of the company's designer Norman Evans. Billiard halls were popular during the Depression. Another leisure facility, across Claremont Road, was the Trocadero building, housing a theatre and later the Arcadia or Trocadero picture house, which closed in the 1980s. Originally Holy Trinity parish hall occupied this site. All are now demolished.

Below: Gilbody's cottage, now demolished, on Wilmslow Road, near Moor Street and the corner of Pill Row (later Stein Place), near the Congregational church. This thatched cottage adjoined two other low-roofed cottages, which were demolished in around 1910. Four other thatched cottages at the corner of Pill Row were cleared for constructing the Congregational church.

Wilmslow Road, Rusholme.

Rusholme Congregational church on the west side of the main road in 1905. Next door used to run Stone (late Stein) Place, named after Doctor Stein who built houses here and was famous for the pills he sold. Opposite lies the Birch Villa Hotel next to Dickenson Road, plus a row of shops, which at that time included a servants' registry office.

A view of a similar date showing the row of houses by the Congregational church, ending at Platt Lane by the park. At that time large houses, with gardens screened by trees, stretched all along here, including Gordon House and the Elms, home to a surgeon. By the 1920s the Casino buildings covered the site, housing shops below, a ballroom, café and also the Casino Cinematograph Theatre until a fire destroyed it in 1962.

WILMSLOW ROAD,

Telephone :
4661 Rusholme

RUSHOLME,

MANCHESTER *February 17*th 1933

Mr Smethurst I.

Dr.to Rusholme Gardens Ltd.

Feby 11 A/c Rendered. £ 20 12 8.

Above: A billhead addressed to Mr Smethurst at Rusholme Gardens, Wilmslow Road, in 1933. This was a rent bill for his flat in Rusholme Gardens, a block of flats opened in 1923. They adjoined the Casino buildings, replacing Melbourne House, on the corner of Platt Lane and having a fine view over Platt Fields. There were thirty service flats and below was a branch of the Manchester & County Bank, a gentlemen's outfitter's and Roy Clarke's sports shop.

Right: Edward Morris, a man blind from birth, on Wilmslow Road in the early 1900s. Daily he stood on Wilmslow Road for fifty-four years. He could describe the early housing and recall people and places of the past, including the rush cart procession, Morris Dancers and the early Cheadle bus services.

Hardy's Well public house on the corner of Dickenson Road (left), originally named the Birch Villa Hotel after the local landowners, as too was Dickenson Road. It served Hardy's ales. It stands opposite Platt Fields with this eye-catching poem on its side wall. In 1901 Norman Wilkinson was the landlord followed by Richard Wood in 1920, Edward Thomas in 1929 and Jonathon Durkan in 1945. Next door used to stand Lesley's Pavilion (see p. 116).

THE THREE-HORSE OMNIBUS, 1856

A three-horse omnibus setting out from the Birch Villa Hotel in 1856. This could carry seventeen passengers inside and twenty-five outside. Ladies travelled inside only. Owned by Mr Wood, it ran from Rusholme, starting at the Birch Villa Hotel. Later there were Scotch plaid painted omnibuses of Scotsman Mr Macewen. The London coach also operated several times a week.

Above: The Cheadle bus in 1910. The driver is James Telford, nicknamed 'Scotch Bob', who drove it for forty years. The Cheadle Omnibus Co. plied between Rusholme and Cheadle and later between Northenden and Cheadle. It had competition from the more modern horse trams of the Manchester Carriage Co.

Right: An advertisement for Holt's luxury coach travel of Wilmslow Road in 1948. They operated from Platt Terrace as did Fingland's Coach Co. Platt Terrace, together with its neighbours, was demolished in 1950. Fingland's Coach Co. now occupies the site.

A mounting block outside Platt Cottage, *c.* 1910. The cottage adjoined Platt Abbey and, together with Platt House and Platt Terrace, stood opposite Platt Fields, between the Birch Villa Hotel and Norman Road. Platt Cottage was home to a wine merchant and then a solicitor in the 1880s. The mounting block was moved there from Poplar House in the early 1900s. Poplar House, dated 1788, stood on Wilmslow Road opposite Thurloe Street.

A blue plaque to the novelist, soldier and playwright Major John Hay Beith, known as Ian Hay, 1876–1952. He wrote over fifty novels and plays. This plaque, attached to Platt Court, a modern block of flats, marks the site of Gothic-style Platt Abbey, where Ian Hay was born. Two blocks of flats called Worsley and Platt Court occupy the site, opposite Platt Fields, on the east side of Wilmslow Road.

Brighton House, Wilmslow Road with Brighton Grove on the right and Norman Road to the left. Facing Platt Fields, this house was one of the few built to the ambitious design for Brighton Grove in 1834. In the 1920s the Kenyons lived here but by 1945 it was a base of the Liverpool Victoria Friendly Society right through to the 1980s. Now it houses Space Computers.

One wing of the flats called Appleby Lodge, opposite Platt Fields. It covers the site of former large houses on Wilmslow Road. In the 1920s Appleby Lodge was a large house lived in by Miss Lilian Ratcliffe, followed in 1929 by Geoffrey Brooke. The house was intended as one of a pair by a lake at the south-west end of the Brighton Grove scheme. By the mid-1930s these ninety-nine flats were on the site.

Above: A blue plaque relating to Sir John Barbirolli on the front northern block of Appleby Lodge. Between 1943 and 1962 Sir John occupied flat No. 79, while he was the popular conductor of the Hallé Orchestra in the city. At No. 87 lived William Royce engineer.

Right: A bust of Sir John Barbirolli outside the Bridgewater Hall in Manchester.

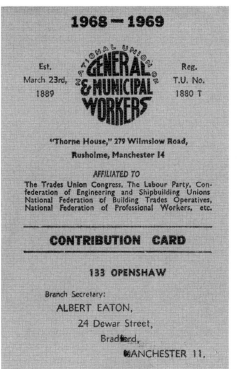

Left: The union contributions card of Frank Rhodes senior, a member of the National Union of General & Municipal Workers, in 1969. The Lancashire general secretary worked in Thorn/Thorne House on Wilmslow Road, next to Appleby Lodge flats.

Opposite above: A plan of 1904 showing the large homes and grounds of the Goldschmitt family at Oldenburg House, plus Westbourne House. Here also was once the Central Evening School of Domestic Economy.

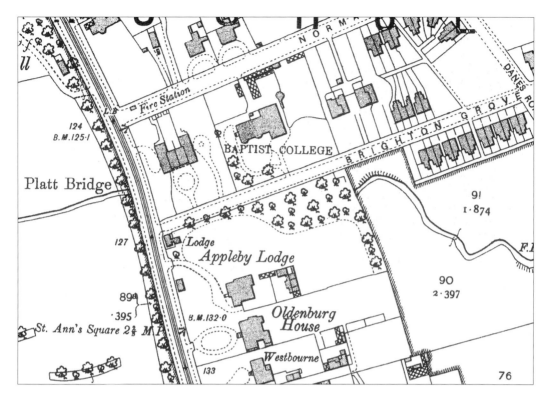

A general view of Wilmslow Road as it passes through the tree-lined southern end of Rusholme, in 1909. On the left lies Platt Fields, Platt Chapel and the large houses of Grangethorpe and Ashfield on the borders of Fallowfield. On the right are the homes of the wealthy with their large ornamental gardens overlooking the park. The original lodge of the Oaks estate lies behind the horse and cart.

The rebuilt lodge of the Oaks, dated 1926, on the corner of Old Hall Lane and Wilmslow Road in 2005. The lodge still guards the entrance but the house is now called Ashburne Hall and is used as halls of residence for the University of Manchester. Here in the lodge, in 1929 lived James Royle, handyman, while Jonathon Hughes lived in the cottage on the estate. By 1945 William O'Callaghan was at the lodge and William Culshaw, handyman, at the cottage.

The Oaks, lying right on the border of Rusholme and Fallowfield and now named Ashburne Hall, in 2005. Designed in the late 1830s by Sir Hubert Worthington for cotton spinning mill owners Robert and Caroline Ogden, it was always known as 'Mr Ogden's House'. It passed to their children and then in around 1869 to Edward Behrens, shipping magnate and MP for Longsight. He left the house and estate to the University of Manchester in 1926.

Ashburne Hall – Mary Worthington Wing – South View   ₩ₙₐₙ. photo. B.

The Mary Worthington hall of residence of Ashburne Hall in the 1920s. In 1926 the university halls of residence at Ashburne House in Victoria Park on Upper Park Road moved here to purpose built halls of residence for women situated in the grounds of the Oaks. A fine dining hall was provided and a library which included the library of Viscount Morley.

Another hall of residence at Ashburne Hall in 2005. The halls are sited around large, lawned areas and the Oaks is off to the left. A long drive, entered from the corner of Old Hall Drive and Wilmslow Road past the lodge, arrives at the Oaks and then opens up into the landscaped halls of residence. Behind this block towers the 'Toast Rack' on Old Hall Lane (see p. 41).

Grangethorpe House on the west side of Wilmslow Road and next to Platt Fields, in 1928. Originally farmland called Bleak Flatt and part of the Platt estate, this half-timbered, gabled house was built in the mid-1800s for a wealthy family. Early English in style, it included ornamental gardens and stables. Occupied by Charles Moseley, India rubber manufacturer, and later by Sir Joseph Leigh MP for Stockport and then Herbert Smith Carrington, it was sold in 1916 to the British Red Cross. A First World War shell stands outside the porch.

A tug-of-war contest at Grangethorpe in June 1918. Servicemen being treated at the hospital take part in a morale boosting sports day. In 1919 the Ministry of Pensions took the hospital over from the War Office but in 1929 transferred patients to Leeds and Liverpool. They sold the buildings to Manchester Royal Infirmary on condition that they remain an orthopaedic service.

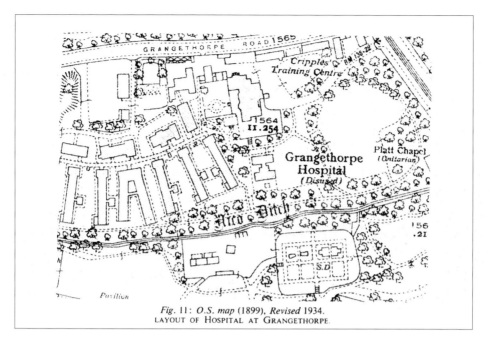

Fig. 11: *O.S. map (1899), Revised 1934.*
LAYOUT OF HOSPITAL AT GRANGETHORPE.

Above and below: A section of a 1934 map showing Grangethorpe as a disused hospital and revealing clearly the layout of the house, grounds and hospital wards. The War Office controlled Grangethorpe Hospital for twelve years with the British Red Cross owning and staffing it, as an orthopaedic military hospital for soldiers wounded during the First World War. Over 7,000 operations were performed here helping to mend 15,000 wounded soldiers and with only 350 deaths. Below is a sports day in 1918.

Sports Day at Grangethorpe in June 1918. There is an interesting array of hat badges, invalid carriages and uniforms here, including the hospital 'blue' of wounded soldiers. Regular sports days were held, one attended by Earl Haig in 1922 and another in 1920 when King George V visited to award medals. The Prince of Wales visited in 1921 to inspect the patients and disabled ex-servicemen, on Platt Fields next door, as so many attended. In 1936 the Infirmary sold the site for £11,000 to Manchester High School for Girls so that they could move out of the city centre and expand (see pp. 112-3).

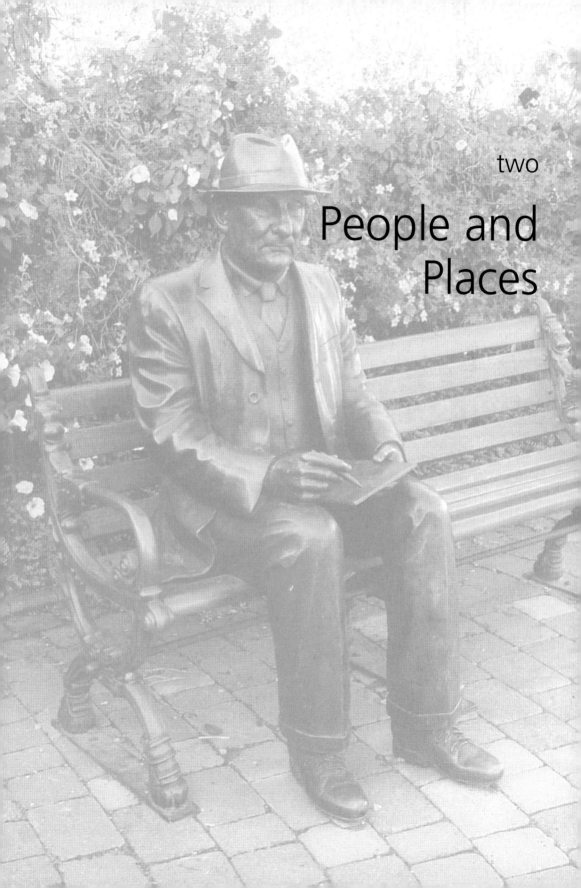

two

People and Places

The ambitious, palatial design of a private company for the Brighton Grove scheme in 1834. It was named after the Prince Regent and Brighton pavilion, because the husband of Elizabeth Worsley (née Norman) was at his court. Norman Road nearby was also named after her family. The aim was to create housing and pleasure gardens around three sides of a quadrangle, centred on a lake formed by Birch (Gore) Brook and crossed by rustic bridges.

Brighton Grove, crossed here by Danes Road, leading to Birch Fields Park and lodge in the distance, *c.* 1907. The road today looks very different from the plan, as only four of the proposed houses had been built on the north side of the road, when the company collapsed. Brighton House is one of the houses, facing Wilmslow Road on the north corner of Brighton Grove. The parish rooms of St James's church are on the right.

Above: The gate posts at the entrance to Brighton Grove are survivors of the original scheme. There was an entrance lodge and an exit lodge, one of which was named Appleby Lodge. The Baptist College was also on Brighton Grove (see pp. 110–11).

Right: The architect William Hardisty lived on the Grove: he designed hospitals and churches, including the Royal Eye Hospital and Christ Church in Moss Side.

Above: Ruggle's cottage on Monmouth Street in the 1880s. Originally known as Granny Lane, it is today Claremont Road and leads westwards off Wilmslow Road. The cottage lay at its junction with John Street (later Holford's Row after John Holford, who built property there and later lived at Rusholme Hall). This unusual, hut-like cottage was demolished in 1884.

Left: The reverse side of a bill for W.M. Holliday's motor car works on Claremont Road in 1933. It reminds the car owner to return his car monthly for servicing, giving different rates for different horse powers. The bill rendered overleaf was for the yearly service and cost £1 3s 6d.

Opposite above: A billhead for council charges for the city of Manchester, payable at the Public Hall on Dickenson Road for 1933-4. The Public Hall and the Reading Room were founded in 1859 and had various homes, opening opposite the Birch Villa Hotel's car park as the Public Free library in 1860. It was used like a community hall and included a museum. They were demolished in 1970.

18167

CITY OF MANCHESTER.

GENERAL RATE, 1933-34. DUE ON DEMAND.
District 17.

J. H. MITCHELL, Collector, attends at the Public Hall Dickenson Road, Mondays, 9 to 12; and Thursdays, 1 to 4.

Mr ROBERT ROE SMETHURST. ....or Occupier,

1.Grd.flr. RUSHOLME GARDENS.WILMSLOW RD.

RUSHOLME. MANCHESTER 14.

Office and Works——————— M ANCHESTER, ————————— 192

HEALD PLACE · RUSHOLME

Also
10 WILMSLOW ROAD &
86 DICKENSON ROAD

TELEPHONE
1158
RUSHOLME

Established 1880

Richard Belt

JOINER · BUILDER
& CONTRACTOR

Above and below: Letter and billheads from the 1920s and 1936 for Richard Belt Ltd, joiner, builder, funeral director and monumental mason. His main works was established in Heald Place in 1880, with other branches following on Wilmslow and Dickenson Roads and in Moston. Heald Place derives from the ancient name of Yielde or Guild House, built on land given in 1224 by the Grelleys to the Hathersage family.

RICHARD BELT Ltd,
Funeral Directors.

❖

Registered Office:
10, WILMSLOW ROAD,
RUSHOLME 14.
Tel. Rusholme 1158.

Directors:
J. E. ORMESHER,
G. E. BASKERVILLE, A.C.A.

Office:
Heald Place, Rusholme,
Manchester 14.

❖

Above: No. 1 Moon Grove with its nameplate, off Dickenson Road, in 2005. Turn into the grove and the short, cobbled road with its period housing is a world away from the bustle of Wilmslow Road. The road has only nine houses. Moon Croft was an early dwelling occupied in 1824 by Thomas Bower.

Left: Dr Adolphe Wahltuch, who lived on Moon Grove, was born in Odessa in Russia in 1837 but came to London and then to Manchester. He worked in various hospitals, including Hulme Dispensary, and was president of several societies, including the Manchester Clinical Society. Author of various publications, he was also a chess expert, becoming president of the Manchester and District Chess League.

No. 2 Moon Grove, a detached house on the north-west corner. During the 1880s and early 1900s James and Sarah Ryder ran a private school here. Up until the 1960s the Ryder family still lived here. No. 4, next door, was used briefly as the rectory by Revd George Greville Anson in the 1840s. It was known as Lilac Villa in the 1880s.

Nos 5 and 7 Moon Grove at its far south-east end. At No. 7 on the right lived an organ builder in the 1880s. By 1920 a Baptist minister occupied the house and by 1929 it was home to the Council of Christian Congregations.

Birch Hall Houses off Old Hall Lane in the early 1900s. Built in the early 1600s with later additions, it was lived in first by the Edge family, supporters of Cromwell. Captain Oliver Edge was a prominent Roundhead. They left in the early eighteenth century. In 1697 the Revd Henry Finch, once of Birch Chapel, preached here at 'a meeting place for an assembly of Protestants dissenting from the Church of England' (see p. 106).

Birch Fold Cottage on Old Hall Lane in the early 1900s. This thatched, black and white timbered cottage was reached off the drive to Birch Hall Farm. This was possibly the oldest cottage in Rusholme and was once moated, but it was demolished in 1912.

Cottrill's cottage painted by Raymond Dearn in 1892. Miss Cottrill lived at Birch Fold Cottage for over fifty years in the late 1800s to early 1900s. Probably it is her standing in the doorway. It was claimed that Cromwell slept there and that an underground tunnel led under the Nico Ditch (see p. 66) to Birch Hall.

'The Toast Rack' on the Hollings college campus of the Manchester Metropolitan University. It was opened in 1960 to a design by L.C. Howitt, as a centre for catering and fashion students. It lies where Birchfield House once stood, between Cromwell Range on the north and Old Hall Lane to the south. New blocks of flats now also stand on the sites of Oak Lawn and Birch Heys, once large houses on Cromwell Range.

Above: A statue of the painter L.S. Lowry, erected in the centre of Mottram-in-Longdendale near Hyde in 2005. Laurence Stephen Lowry was born in Old Trafford in 1887 but came to live in Rusholme at an early age. He attended school at Victoria Park between 1895 and 1904. In 1909 his family moved to Pendlebury. He is best known for his distinctive depictions of Northern mill town life.

Left: This was the childhood home of Lowry at 14 Pine Grove, just off Longford Place. The address was Victoria Park although these later housing developments lie just outside the original select housing estate. His aunt, Mary Lowry, was matron at a charitable home on Rusholme Road and another aunt, Annie, ran a glass and china shop on Wilmlsow Road.

Above: Looking along Platt Lane towards Wilmslow Road in 1908. On the right are the railings of Platt Fields and on the left the walls and fencing of large, elegant houses overlooking the park. The leafy lane is quite rural looking and in the distance was once a village nightwatchman's wooden hut, from which he would announce the time of day and the weather.

Below: A billhead of A.O. Holt, electrical engineer, of Platt Works on Platt Lane in 1932. His bill is directed to a resident in the apartments at Rusholme Gardens on the north corner of Platt Lane, at its junction with Wilmslow Road. In the 1920s Mr Holt provided ' high-class electric lighting, bells and telephones'.

Telephone :
RUSHOLME 1204.

PLATT WORKS,

Platt Lane, Rusholme,

MANCHESTER, 1st March 1932.

Mr R Smethurst, No 1 Flat, Rusholme Gardens.

Dr. to A. O. HOLT,

ELECTRICAL ENGINEER.

Terms : NETT.

Speciality : High-Class Electric Lighting, Bells and Telephones.

29/2/32. To supplying and fitting 2. 230 Volt 1000 Watt "Sullivan"
complete elements in electric fire. @ 12/3 each. £1   4   6

Appleby House on Platt Lane, lying between Grove and Taylor Streets. It was built in the late 1800s for Frederick Appleby, a civil engineer, who lived there until the 1890s. By 1901 Edwin Holt, a solicitor and local councillor (1893-1904), was the occupant. In the 1960s it became a hostel for students of Domestic Science at Hollings College, and today is the Nigeria Centre, with a restaurant called Out of Africa.

Part of a row of houses on Platt Lane, facing Platt Fields and the church of Holy Trinity. On the right runs Grove Street, next to this matching pair of houses known as Elton Bank. Off to the left is Glen House, which is also part of a matching pair with The Lodge next door to it.

Rusholme Gardens Private Hotel

Platt Lane, Wilmslow Road, Rusholme, Manchester

M _A. Smethurst._   I   *Week ending* October 7th 1933

	SUN. £ s. d.	MON. £ s. d.	TUES. £ s. d.	WED. £ s. d.	THURS. £ s. d.	FRI. £ s. d.	SAT. £ s. d.	TOTAL £ s. d.
Apartments								
Food								
Breakfast		1 3	1 3					2 6
Lunch								
Tea	6	6	6					1 6
Dinner								
Supper	2 3	2 3						4 6
Milk								
Minerals		10						10
Coal & Wood								
Laundry								
Paid Out								
Sundries								
								9 4
							Sept 23/ a/c Rd	1-3 7
								1-12-11

Above: A bill for the Rusholme Gardens private hotel in 1933. No. 1 Elton Bank became a private hotel and continues today as the Elton Bank Hotel. In the 1880s Thomas Ashton, commercial agent, lived here, followed by Edward Salomons and in 1929 the rector of St Ann's church in the city of Manchester.

Right: Edward Salomons, architect, 1828–1906. Between 1893 and 1906 he lived in retirement at No. 1 Elton Bank. As an architect Edward designed his own homes in Victoria Park at the Cottage and at the Gables, as well as designing many public buildings and houses in Manchester, London and elsewhere.

Glen or Glenn House, at 64 Platt Lane, was home to John Louden, a shipper, from the 1880s until around 1910. In 1920 George Booth lived there and in 1929 Isaac Davis, a cabinet maker. It was built together with its twin the Lodge in around 1836 by Mr Ainsworth, who then lived in Glen House.

The Lodge at 66 Platt Lane, where John Moscrop, engineer, lived in the 1890s to early 1900s. By 1909 his widow Caroline was living there alone. She stayed there until the 1920s. Platt Lane ended here originally, being known as Platt Grove. The road was widened, taking away the wide sweep of the drives to these houses.

Above: The Nook at 68 Platt Lane, where Robert Pickup, a chemist, lived during the 1880s into the early 1900s. William Haslam, a coal merchant, resided there from around 1909 through to the late 1920s. It was built in about 1838 and like the rest of the row had stables in its grounds.

Right: Advertisements for the Manchester & Salford Equitable Co-operative Society emporium on Platt Lane, established in 1924. This large store was the Co-op's grocery section, situated between Tintern Street and Yew Tree Road on the north side of Platt Lane. In the centre is an advertisement from 1980 for the upstairs ballroom used by a dancing school.

CAPRI BALLROOM

(Derek & Susan Young)

School of Dancing

Platt Lane, (Over Co-op), Rusholme, Tel: 224-2485

MONDAY: Doors open 7.45pm—Ballroom & Latin Dancing
TUESDAY: RESERVED FOR PRIVATE LESSONS
WEDNESDAY: Doors open 7.45pm—Disco Class
FRIDAY: Doors open 8.00pm—Ballroom & Latin Dancing
8.00—11.00 Advanced dancers & competitors, practice night.
SATURDAY: Doors open 8.00pm for: Social Ballroom & Latin Dancing till 11.00pm.
JUNIOR BALLROOM DANCING CLASSES Saturday morning: 11.00—12.30

NEW ADULT & JUNIOR COURSES COMMENCING:
MONDAY 9th JUNE; SATURDAY 13th JUNE.
TWO LARGE ROOMS ★ TWO LICENSED BARS AVAILABLE FOR PRIVATE PARTIES, BUFFET DANCES, WEDDINGS, ETC.

A view of Summer Place in the 1940s, which runs parallel with Platt Lane and off which lead Nelson
(later Victory) and Grove Streets. Like Nelson Place, here was older terraced housing, cleared away for
modern council estates. Sir Neville Cardus (1889-1975), who was born at No. 2 in 1889, describes
the exterior and interior of these houses and his neighbours in his autobiography. Journalist, critic and
commentator, he had attended the local board school. His love of literature, music and cricket resulted in
him working for the *Manchester Guardian* until 1939 and then living and working in both Australia and
London. Renowned for his cricket commentaries, his music critiques and his love of literature, as well
for his speaking and correspondence, he was knighted in 1967.

Above: The Osborne House public house on the corner of the passageway known as Wood's Buildings West and Victory (late Nelson) Street, which joins Summer Place on the left. The public house was leased by Hydes brewery in 1889, bought by them in 1904 and their beer is still sold there today. This public house is part of the earlier Rusholme with its older terraced housing.

Right: The Gardeners' Arms public house further along Victory Street. Nelson Street, Place and Square (nicknamed 'Hell Square') bore nameplates dated 1843. The area was named after Lord Nelson by an old soldier, who in the 1800s lived at the bottom of Moor Street and owned some of the land. Much of this early housing was cleared away to make room for council housing, leaving just the public houses.

Above: The Welcome public house off Rusholme Grove. The building faces away from the Grove into the court. The walls of the public house held photographs of its famous clientele. Here actors from the nearby film studios, and later the BBC studios (see pp 118-120), came to socialise. So too did the conductor and musicians of the BBC Northern Light orchestra.

Left: One of the stained glass windows of the Welcome public house. The Art Deco style windows proclaim the now defunct brewery of Groves and Whitnall but now the public house serves Greenall's beer. The smoke room recalls the days of the parlour, lounge and snug rooms once found in a public house.

Above: Carter's Lache, one of three cottages set back from Rusholme Green near Thurloe Street. 'Lache' is another word for 'lake'. The cottages were black and white timbered and thatched. Here at No. 1 Archie Wilson lived. In the *Manchester Mercury* for 1752 the cottage was for sale with thirty-seven acres, with George Booth as owner and Samuel Burrough as tenant.

Right: Archie Wilson, a cobbler, wearing his stock-in-trade top hat, in the early 1900s. One of five brothers, he was fond of his drink and quite a philosopher, even quarrelling with his pet raven.

Walmer Street in the 1920s. The street lies off Wilmslow Road running to Santiago Street. At its junction with Albert Street is the Albert Inn. This public house was bought by Hydes brewery in 1890. Almost opposite was the Crown Inn on the corner of Blundell Street. Today only the Albert Inn survives of these earlier buildings.

A advertisement for the Golden Vale Farm Dairy at 60 Walmer Street in 1911. It also had a branch on Great Western Street off Wilmslow Road.

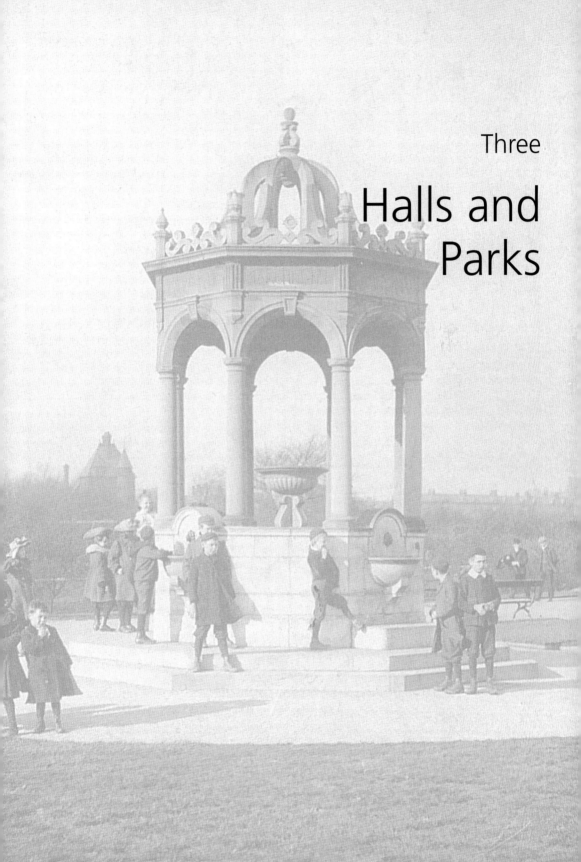

Three

Halls and Parks

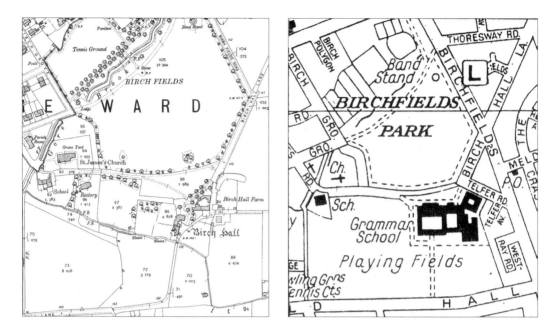

Above, left and right: Two plans of the Birch Hall estate in 1904 and in the 1950s, showing its transformation from a hall set in acres of woodland with probably a large manorial corn mill into a public park. The hall and its adjacent farm were demolished in 1926 for the new home of Manchester Grammar School.

A painting of Birch Hall by Raymond Dearn in 1892. The estate, originally called Hindley Birches, covered well over thirty acres and was given by the Hathersage family to Matthew de Birches in 1190. It is bordered by Gore Brook on the north-west and Nico Ditch on the south.

Above: Birch Hall in the early 1900s. The back section is the original black and white half-timbered building. The front with its entrance porch was added along with other additions through the 1700s and 1800s. Originally the site was moated and trees sheltered the hall, which was approached from Old Hall Lane or Birch Hall Lane. In 1926 it was demolished and now Manchester Grammar School and its grounds cover the site.

Right: The Birch family coat of arms. The family of Colonel Thomas Birch, Parliamentarian and Non-conformist, 1608-1678, owned and lived at Birch Hall until 1743 and John Dickinson (hence Dickenson Road) bought the estate in around 1745. Later the Ansons (hence Anson Road) acquired the hall through marriage. John Dickinson was a Manchester merchant and landowner in Rusholme, whose mother's maiden name was Birch. He brought with him from his city home its two gateposts and the bed Prince Charles the Pretender slept in.

BIRCH of Birch. *A-zure three fleurs de lis argent.*

Birch Hall Farm in 1904. The farm lay near the hall together with its barns and farmyard pond. Five generations of the Ratcliffe family farmed there from 1679, hence its other name, 'Ratcliffe's Farm'. In 1926 they moved on to farm at Styal when the site was sold and cleared to make way for the grammar school.

In 1888 Birch Fields public park was opened by Prince Albert Victor presented with a gold key by Alderman Chesters Thompson. In 1887 Herbert Philips had bought four and a half acres adjoining Dickenson Road as a playground, thus gaining access from Dickenson Road. Manchester Corporation bought most of the thirty-three acres from the trustees of Richard Cobden MP and from Sir William Anson, who himself donated five more acres.

The north-east lodge of Birch Fields Park at the Dickenson Road entrance, 1912. There were two lodges, the other sited on the west side off Brighton and Birch Groves. Birchfields Road runs here along the right hand side of the park. Inside this main gate were herbaceous borders and a rose garden. There was also an 'elderly men's rest' or shelter, children's playground and playing fields.

The Avenue in Birch Fields Park in 1916. This long walk ran between Gore Brook on the right and the sports ground on the left. The walk was lined with lime trees and edged with shrubs. It ran north-eastwards from the western lodge to the bandstand and so on to the lodge at Dickenson Road.

The Avenue or Favourite Walk in 1914. The avenue runs north-eastwards through Birch Fields Park and on the left are the eight tennis courts. There were also two bowling greens and two cricket pitches north of the tennis ground.

The bandstand on the north side of Birch Fields Park near its perimeter by Birchfields Road. It ended the walk along the Avenue and was close to the main lodge but, sadly, it has been demolished. During the Second World War a barrage balloon was sited near here to stop low flying bombers and dive bombing.

A footbridge over the Gore Brook in 1906. In the distance is the bandstand north of the bridge. It lay about halfway along the Favourite Walk, connecting the sports areas and walk with the rest of Birch Fields Park.

The Gore Brook, also known as Birch Brook, with the bandstand in the distance, in the early 1900s. The landscaping made use of the ancient brook to bisect Birch Fields Park and to add a natural feature to the park.

The footbridge across Gore Brook giving access to the fountain and the large stone, in 1906. This huge, sandstone boulder stone, weighing thirteen tons, was found in 1898 by the building contractors, Messrs Etheridge & Clark, who presented it to Birch Fields Park as a curiosity for visitors. It was discovered by them during the culverting of Gore Brook under Hamilton Road sixteen feet down. It still stands in the park today.

The fountain near the boulder stone in 1906. This drinking fountain was one of several erected in Birch Fields Park from a bequest left by Alderman Clay.

L.O.3.   THE BRIDGE AND TENNIS COURTS, BIRCH PARK, MANCHESTER.

The boulder stone, with children standing near the footbridge over Gore Brook; beyond it are the tennis courts. Tucked away is the pavilion or kiosk serving refreshments. At the south-west corner of Birch Fields Park lies St James's church, Birch with its rectory and schools. A large field behind the schools was used in the early 1910s as an exhibition area until the exhibition halls were destroyed in a fire.

A stroll in Birch Fields Park in the 1910s. On the left is the band stand.

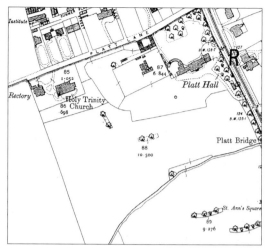

Above, right and left: Two plans showing Platt Hall and estate in 1904 and the hall and public park forming Platt Fields in the 1950s. Now covering ninety acres, the park is bordered by Platt Lane on the north and north-west, Yew Tree Road on the west and Wilmslow Road to the east, stretching into Fallowfield to the south. The word Platt is Anglo-Saxon meaning 'sheepfold'. In 1190 these lands were conveyed to the Knights of St John, who rented the land and hall to a family, who took its name Platt.

Platt Hall with a statue of Abraham Lincoln in front, in 1958. This is the third hall, tucked in the north-east corner of the estate. The earliest probably dated back to the Crusades and then a black and white timbered hall was built in the gardens of the present hall, at right angles to Wilmslow Road. This was demolished in around 1764; it included, 'the hall, great parlor, the buttery, the milk-house, the woman's parlor, the little parlor, the brew house, the kitchen with Bessy parlor, the drinkhouse, the cheese chamber' and other accommodation.

THE HALL, PLATT FIELDS, MANCHESTER.

Above: Platt Hall in 1938. In 1625 the estate was sold to a merchant Ralph Worsley for £550. In 1764 John and Deborah Carill-Worsley built this Georgian hall with landscaped gardens for £10,000. Red bricks soaked in oil made the outer walls appear brighter. The Ionic pillared, stone portico entrance sits at the centre of this symmetrical design, with a kitchen wing on one side and stable block on the other. A cobbled yard and outbuildings, plus a lodge on Wilmslow Road, completed the plan.

Right: Major General Charles Worlsey, 1622-1656. His grandfather Charles employed hand loom weavers and probably stored the woven fabric at Platt Hall. Charles' father Ralph, a Puritan and textile merchant bought Platt Hall. Charles, also a Puritan, in 1650, aged only twenty-eight, raised a muster of soldiers to fight for Cromwell. He helped to remove the mace when the Long Parliament was dissolved, becoming Manchester's first MP in 1654. He died in London aged only thirty-five and is buried in Westminster Abbey.

Platt Hall for sale in 1906. Its owners tried unsuccessfully to sell off the estate in 1901 and 1906 by public auction. In 1907 some small plots were sold, destined for shops and houses and the hall was to be demolished to provide bricks for the housing. The old woodland was to be torn up. Public feeling about the impending loss ran high and William Royle led a campaign, canvassing and leafleting the town, in an attempt to save the estate for Rusholme.

'William Royle of Rusholme' in 1914. He organised a public meeting and won public support plus the Lord Mayor's approval. More than eighty acres were bought for £59,875 by Manchester Corporation, including the plot already sold. The public raised £3,000 to buy back the sold plot in 1907 but in the end the corporation paid for it. In 1927 the hall became home to the Manchester City Art Gallery of English Costume.

Above: A memorial seat to William Royle in Platt Fields near Wilmslow Road, paid for by public subscription in 1924. A true Rusholmite, he loved the town, was a deeply religious Wesleyan lay preacher and an active Liberal, wishing to help the downtrodden and his home town. He was born in 1854, he lived on Moor Street and attended Birch infant and Platt day schools, and continued to educate himself throughout his life. After marriage he lived on Duke Street and later at Elmwood on Birch Polygon. He published *The History of Rusholme* in 1905. He died in 1923 and was buried in Birch church yard.

Right: The gatepost to Ashfield on Wilmslow Road, just on the border with Fallowfield, near Platt Chapel. Occupied first by a Manchester merchant Mr Robinson and last by Thomas Aitkin's widow, its ten and a half acres of estate was bought for Rusholme by Edward Donner in 1913. Added to Platt Fields, it made the park ninety-one and a half acres altogether. Only the gatepost remains now and in its grounds stand some of the remains of windows from Manchester Cathedral, removed during alterations.

Platt bridge passing over Platt (Gore) Brook near Nico Ditch in Platt Fields. Gore Brook was an ancient boundary in the 1190 conveyance of land to the Knights of St John, being the confluence of the Moss, Dick Lane and Dodgeleach brooks and culverted at many points. Here once up to thirty yards wide with a tiled basin, it was used for skating and swimming and was originally strong enough to power a manorial corn mill. Nico Ditch was probably a defensive ditch raised in Anglo Saxon times as a defence by King Offa and often forming a boundary line.

Making the boating lake in Platt Fields in 1908/9. With so many unemployed it was decided to use some of the surplus labour to create a lake. The Local Government Board lent some money and gave a grant. Throughout the winter of 1908/9 seven hundred and twenty men dug out six and a half acres to form the lake, assisted in this labour only by horses and carts.

The opening of the park and lake at Platt Fields in 1910. The Lord Mayor Sir Charles Behrens, together with invited dignitaries, takes the first tour by launch across the lake. Seated by him, wearing a bowler hat, is William Royle. Crowds lined the banks of the lake. Sir Charles opened the park and William Royle made the opening speech.

By the lake at Platt Fields in 1924. Across the water is an island with a small bay and sanctuary for wild fowl on its southern side. The lake formed the south-west corner of the park, where Yew Tree Road runs along the west edge of the park.

The boathouse and landing stage at Platt Fields lake in 1910. One of the launches used was called *The Archie Littlemore*. There were also special ponds for model yacht enthusiasts.

John Hynes, aged about nine, one Sunday in around 1954. His parents took him to Platt Fields Park to ride his prized (second-hand) bicycle in safety. His father Jack snapped him by the lake with its island sanctuary.

The children's paddling pool in Platt Fields in the 1920s. In the 1950s a children's club was held near the lake at 'Sunshine Corner'. The verse went: 'Sunshine Corner – oh, it's very fine, All for children under ninety-nine, All are welcome, seats are given free, Sunshine Corner is the place for me'.

A statue of Abraham Lincoln outside Platt Hall in 1991. Designed by George Grey Barnard, it was presented to Manchester in 1919 by Mr and Mrs Charles Taft of Cincinnati, Ohio, in recognition of the support of their Lancashire friends to Lincoln's cause and to the suffering of the cotton workers during the cotton famine, when ports were blockaded in the Southern States. The statue now stands in Lincoln Square off Deansgate in the city centre.

A busy, fine day in Platt Fields park in the 1910s. The spire of Holy Trinity church is in the background, lying on the north side of the park off Platt Lane. Many different kinds of events have been held in the park over the years. In July 1937 Manchester and Salford Peace Week celebrated the end of the First World War with a procession to Platt Fields. Over a hundred women's organisations celebrated 'Women's Day'. Various pageants have been staged, such as the 1938 city's centenary celebrations and more recently it has been the venue for Manchester's popular 'Garden of Delights' festivals.

PUBLIC ENTRANCES TO ROYAL LANCASHIRE SHOW, PLATT FIELDS (Rusholme), MANCHESTER,
Thursday, July 30th, to Monday (Bank Holiday), August 3rd, inclusive.

The entrances to the Royal Lancashire show at Platt Fields in 1908. The Agricultural Society held their show over the former Bank holiday weekend at the beginning of August. Here also was held the first purely electrical exhibition for the area in October 1908. In 1919 a tank from the First World War was placed in the park, presented by the National War Savings committee.

The Shakespearean garden in Platt Fields park in the 1930s. Here in the former walled garden of Ashfield, herbs, flowers and plants mentioned in Shakespeare's plays are grown in a pleasant garden design. In 2002 the Jubilee gardens were established for Queen Elizabeth's Jubilee year. The fountain from Piccadilly Gardens in the city centre was placed in front of Platt Hall.

Slade Hall on Slade Lane. The Slade estate, dating back to the 1200s, was owned by a Manchester family who adopted the local name Slade. In the 1580s it became home to the Siddall (Syddall) family. The present timber-framed hall was built in the sixteenth century, with later additions. The estate lay in Gorton and in Rusholme (including the hall) but is nowadays more usually referred to as in Longsight.

The Rusholme gate entrance to Whitworth Park, off Moss Lane East and Wilmslow Road, in the early 1900s. The park covers twenty-five acres of Rusholme and Chorlton-on-Medlock, with two gates on Oxford Road. On the death of Joseph Whitworth, whose engineering works in Openshaw produced machine tools and armaments, his trustees bought 'Potter's Field/Park' in 1888, which belonged to the Entwistle family of Rusholme House.

A special day by the lake in Whitworth Park in 1906. The park adjoins the Whitworth Institute in Grove House, which opened as an art gallery in 1890 and was redesigned in 1908 by Beaumont. In 1905 all this park and institute (on the left) were presented to the city of Manchester. The Union Baptist chapel lies in the background on Oxford Road. There was a meteorological observatory on the far side of the lake.

The Whitworth Art Gallery in Whitworth Park after its redesign and with a statue of King Edward VII, 1913. This bronze statue was sculpted by John Cassidy and presented in 1913 to the city of Manchester by James Gresham Mice JP, an art collector and engineer. The flower beds once surrounding it were later removed.

The statue of King Edward VII in 1916 was originally intended as a memorial for Piccadilly in the city to the Lord Mayor Sir Charles Behrens but it was placed in the park near the Oxford Road entrance, facing the Manchester Royal Infirmary which the King had officially opened.

A statue called 'Christ Blessing the Children', set in flower beds, in Whitworth park in 1910. The Whitworth Art Gallery lies behind. This statue was installed in 1895 and was the first major commissioned sculpture for a Manchester city park. The terracotta group of Christ with three children was designed by George Tinworth and was the gift of one of Whitworth's trustees, R.D. Darbyshire (see p. 86).

The same statue seen in Whitworth Park in 1905. On the right is the Union Baptist chapel. The statue was damaged during the Second World War, either by vandals or by a barrage balloon, and was removed for storage. It has consequently been lost but the pedestal stayed in place for fifty years before it was removed. Its inscription read: 'Jesus said, "Let the little children come unto me".'

The Avenue and archway in Whitworth park in 1907. The park contained many flower beds, tree-lined walks and open grassed areas, as well as a children's playground and lake. On the right is the tower and spire of the Union Baptist chapel on Oxford Road. On the left lies the Whitworth Institute.

Flower beds in Whitworth park in 1911. Behind is the Union Baptist chapel on Oxford Road. Centre left is the statue of Christ blessing the children. There were three statues set up in the park: this one, Edward VII and in 1908 a figure with a sun dial was presented by the executors of Mrs Entwistle, whose family had owned the land.

The Lake in Whitworth park and Whitworth Art Gallery in the background in the early 1900s. The lake, sited in the south-west corner of the park near Parker Street, had islands with rocks and bushes on as a sanctuary for birds. On the right is the meteorological observatory.

Children by the lake in Whitworth park in 1905. Housing on Parker Street can be seen on the right. The park is bounded by Acomb and Parker Streets on the west, Moss Lane East on the south, Oxford Road to the east and Denmark Road on the north.

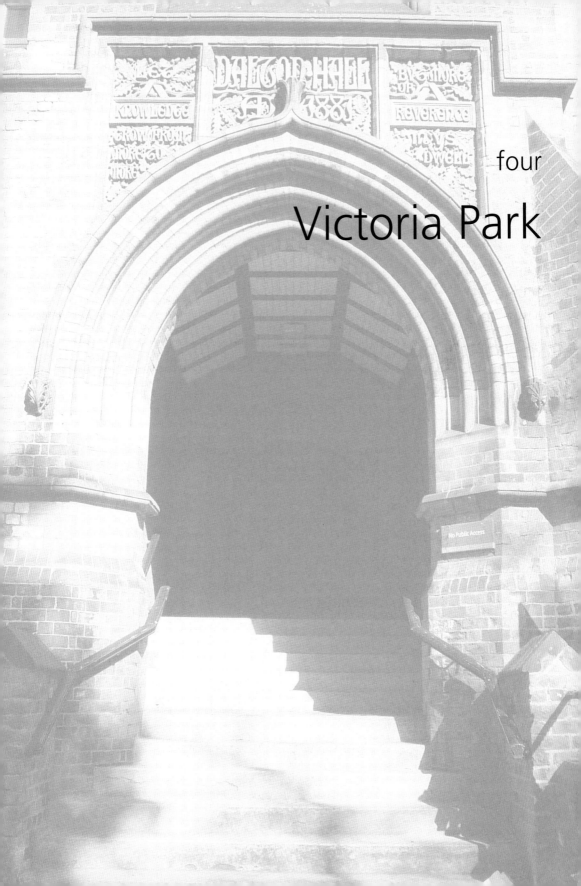

four

Victoria Park

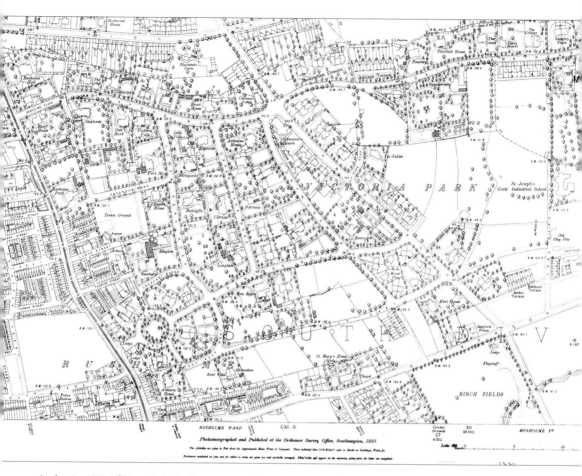

A plan in 1899 of Victoria Park, the concept of the Victoria Park Company in 1836. An Act of Parliament in 1837 allowed them to open in July with 146 acres of land, covering Rusholme, Longsight, the detached part of Moss Side and Chorlton-on-Medlock. Much of the land formed part of the Birch estate of the Dickinson family. The method was speculative: to let or sell building plots/houses and the architect was Richard Lane. Only nine of the houses were constructed, when the company folded in 1839. In 1845 the Victoria Park Trust resurrected the scheme and the park developed steadily: by 1850 there were sixty-five houses with three hundred and ninety residents and in 1899, one hundred and twenty-eight houses.

Opposite below: The Longsight entrance into Victoria Park in the early 1900s. This also contains the regulations, fine lamps and railings and a hut for the toll keeper. The castellated gates lead into Daisy Bank Road and Plymouth Grove runs across the foreground. Originally this entrance had large, castellated lodges. In 1870 the extension of Plymouth Grove to the north end of Birch Lane had meant the gates being set back from their original position on Stockport Road.

I intended sending P.c. to say it was impossible to take Mabs down on Monda

Above: The south-west entrance at Rusholme Green with its gates and lodges in 1906. The plan was for a private, secluded, healthy estate, with manned toll gates to control entry. Of the various gates the most elaborate were the south-west and the north-west ones, at the Crescent Range and the Oxford Place entrances, both exiting onto Wilmslow Road. The notice on the gates sets out the terms and rules of the Victoria Park Trust. Tolls were exacted from pedestrians, equestrians, carts, bicycles and motor cars with the later trams being free.

Two castellated gateposts surviving from the Longsight entrance on Daisy Bank Road and now erected at the Rusholme entrance. In the north-east corner of the park, they guarded the exit onto Plymouth Grove in Longsight. They are all that remains of the gateways into the park.

Right: The plaque attached to the gatepost at the Rusholme entrance, records the rescue of the last two gates by Manchester City Corporation and the Rusholme and Fallowfield Civic Society in 1987. Both Sir William Anson's opposition to tolls and also trams operating along Anson Road through the estate undermined the effectiveness of the toll gates and they were removed.

Below: Mr Hadfield's House and original-sized garden at No. 2 Conyngham Road. George Hadfield, Liberal MP for Sheffield, Non-Conformist and lawyer, lived here until 1879. Called also 'Mr Hadfield's House in the Park', it is one of the oldest houses and is now converted into apartments. Some of the nine original houses have been demolished, such as Park Villa, the home of the estate's architect Richard Lane, on Oxford Place.

Left: Addison Terrace off Daisy Bank Road, another survivor of the original housing of the 1840s, unlike Addison House next door which was demolished in 1977. These twelve houses were speculative building and housed some interesting and well-known people over the years. In the 1970s they were converted into flats and continue as such.

Below: A close-up of the details on Addison Terrace off Daisy Bank Road. Regency in style, the terrace has Gothic windows with pointed arches reflecting the arched doorways with traceried panels. Statues and carved heads adorn the walls. The white of the walls sets off the architecture perfectly.

Right: A blue plaque above the doorway to No. 3 Addison Terrace. Here lived Charles Hallé from 1848, when he became conductor and founder of the Hallé Orchestra. He rented his furnished home for £12 a month. The Pre-Raphaelite painter Ford Madox Brown also lived at No. 3, between 1883 and 1887, while he painted his famous murals in Manchester Town Hall.

Below: The Victoria Park Hospital on Buckingham Crescent off Daisy Bank Road. The name plate of the crescent survives on the garden wall of the crescent. Like this house, many of the fine houses in the park became home eventually to institutions, specialised hospital departments or nursing and residential homes.

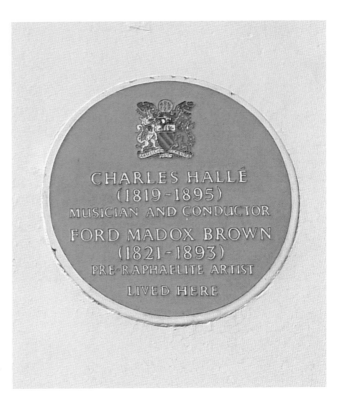

No. 4 Buckingham Crescent, off Daisy Bank Road, where the Pankhurst family lived: Emmeline and her family, including daughters, Christobel and Sylvia, who were famous for their campaign to get the vote for women. Edward Donner, merchant, educationist and politician lived at No. 7 in the 1870s and Elias Bancroft, landscape painter, in the 1890s. At No. 2 was Sir Gerald Hertz (later Hurst), politician and historian.

Hirstwood on Daisy Bank Road, now the Methodist International Home, mostly for foreign students since the 1950s. Edward Salomons the architect built it as his home in 1880. He named it The Cottage and it was renamed Hirstwood by its owner Alfred Kitchen in the early 1900s. The original design and fine quality of both exterior and interior are all still apparent today.

Lily/Lilly Villa and stables, now known as Grey Garth, on Lower Park Road at its junction
with Oxford Place. This grey brick house was home to the family of cotton merchant Philip
Ziegler, together with six servants, from 1865. Their son's death at Gallipoli is recorded on the
war memorial in St Chrysostom's church. His mother Lilly named the house, which is now a
university hall of residence for men under the care of Opus Dei.

Ashburne House on the corner of Oxford Place and Upper Park Road in 1906. Built in 1849, it
was home to William Romaine Callender jnr, manufacturer and MP for Manchester and where he
entertained Disraeli. In 1900 Robert Dukinfield Darbyshire bought it to give it to the university
for a women's hall of residence. It proved too small a site and in 1926 they moved out to The
Oaks off Wilmslow Road (see pp 28–9). Manchester Theological College took it over in the 1930s
as Egerton College.

High Elms on Upper Park Road. Here from 1867 to 1895 lived Robert Dukinfield Darbyshire, who also bought Ashburne House next door to his home. He was associated with Owens College (later the University of Manchester), Manchester High School for Girls and the Whitworth Art Gallery, where his portrait hangs. By 1914, and through to the 1970s, High Elms was a nursing home and it is now a residential home.

Langdale House on the corner of Denison Road and Upper Park Road. This fine, Gothic design is by the architect Henry Bowman, whose initials can be seen on the downspouts. Together with stables at the side, it was built in 1846 for Edward Riley Langworthy, MP for Salford and its mayor, who lived there until 1874. In around 1911 it became a hostel for women students and later added two extensions to its grounds. The University of Manchester sold it in 2002 and it has now become residential apartments.

Above: St Chrysostom's Anglican church on the corner of Anson Road, on the left, and Oxford Place and Conyngham Road, on the right, early 1900s. This busy junction has Daisy Bank Road off to the left and Upper Brook Street running towards the church from Manchester. This church was in the original Victoria Park plan but not built until 1877. The original design was by George Redmayne. A disastrous fire in 1904 caused much damage and it was almost rebuilt in 1906, to a design by John Ely.

Below: The interior of the Roman Catholic church of St Edward on Thurloe Street in 1907. The church and manse lie tucked in the corner at its junction with Crescent Range. Built in 1862 to a design by Edward W. Pugin, it had a long association with the Xaverian Brothers next door (see pp. 91–3).

Above: The exterior of the First Church of Christ Scientist on Daisy Bank Road in 1906. Designed by the architect Edgar Wood, this church is renowned for its striking Arts and Crafts exterior and interior. It opened in 1903 on a green, vacant plot. In 1971 it became disused but in 1976 was restored as an annexe to Elizabeth Gaskell College and nowadays is known as the Edgar Wood Centre.

Left: The Welsh Calvinistic Methodist chapel at the junction of Daisy Bank Road and Longford Place. Opened in 1928 it bears a dedication in both English and Welsh. Today it is home to the Victoria Park Christian Fellowship.

Summerville House on Daisy Bank Road. The park was home to a few religious training colleges. Summerville housed the Unitarian Home Missionary Society's Theological College and hall of residence for men from 1905 for up to eighty years. It is one of the original houses of the park plan and one of the largest and grandest. It was home from 1857 to 1858 to Sir Harry and Lady Juana Smith: he was a governor and soldier in South Africa and she gave her name to Ladysmith.

The stable block of Summerville, which bears a plaque in Latin recording the time of the Unitarians: '1923 Where the spirit of the Lord is, there is Freedom'. William Kessler, a German merchant, and family lived in Summerville between 1859 and 1904. Its grounds once stretched across Daisy Bank Road. Summerville became a hall of residence for the university in the 1980s and is now residential apartments.

Above: The Free Methodist College by the Rusholme gateway on Crescent Range, 1905. The building still stands and was three houses adapted in 1877 into a Theological College by the United Methodist Free Churches. A new wing was added in 1896 and in 1907 the college was united with Ranmoor College in Sheffield. Used as a Voluntary Aid Detachment hospital during the First World War, it joined with Hartley College in 1919 and, after a further union with Didsbury College, closed in 1934.

Left: The fine red brick entrance to Dalton Hall off Conyngham Road. The text is by the poet Tennyson and reflects the Quaker and Pacifist beliefs of the founders, who chose John Dalton as the college's namesake. The architect was George Redmayne, who also designed St Chrysostom's church next door and the style of architecture is Arts and Crafts.

Dalton Hall lying between Anson and Conyngham Roads, 1903. This was opened in 1881 by the Quakers so that their students could attend Owens College (later the University of Manchester). The college fronts right onto the pavement with no grounds in between.

Firwood House on Lower Park Road. Originally called Blagdon, it was designed for Thomas Hetherington in the 1870s by the architect Alfred Waterhouse. It opened in 1907 as Xaverian College run by the Roman Catholic Xaverian Brothers. Renamed Firwood in the 1890s, it forms the main building of the college, which has extensions and new buildings in the grounds of Firwood, as well as other houses in the park.

Sunbury House on the corner of Thurloe Street and Park Crescent. This house was home to three merchants: Otho Horkeimer in the early 1880s, Harry Lazarus in the late 1880s and then Philip Kessler from around 1895 until 1907. Xaverian College took this house over and it now stands within the college complex.

Marylands House on Lower Park Road in 1911. This was home from the 1870s to Edmund Potter Liberal MP, Sir Henry Roscoe, professor at the university and the merchant Louis Grommé. This yellow brick house has detailed tiling on its exterior and a fine interior. In 1930 Xaverian College took over this house, now renamed Regent House, and its garden provides a sports area.

Saville House on Lower Park Road. This Italianate, imposing house was home to the Leisler family and then East India merchant, William Gaddum, who called it Stoneywood. Up until 1919 the perfume merchant Adolphe Saalfeld lived here. He was a survivor of the *Titanic* sinking, along with his perfume samples. Renamed Ward Hall the building has housed students from various colleges since 1919 and now forms part of Xaverian College.

St Joseph's Convent Central School on Laindon (late Victoria) Road in the early 1900s. It was run by the nuns of Charity of St Vincent de Paul. It was sold and became a Central School and later St Joseph's Technical School.

The architect's drawing for two houses on Longford Place in 1881. During the late 1800s empty plots were filled in by smaller houses, often referred to as cottages. New roads were gradually introduced with rows of semi-detached and terraced housing. Longford Place is just on the edge of the original park and joins Daisy Bank Road where the Welsh Calvinist Methodist chapel stands. It had semi-detached houses like these and also terraced housing.

Chadlington House on Daisy Bank Road on the corner of Scarsdale Road. The road was a later development of houses and this turretted house is a fine later addition to the park. It was architect designed in 1914. Here lived Ernest Bosden Leech, who compiled the centenary account of Victoria Park in 1937.

Park Wood Terrace, built in the late 1880s, on Daisy Bank Road. This row of tall terraced housing is another example of the later additions to the original scheme. Next door are the five houses of Woodlands, built at a similar time.

The cottage and coach house to South Villa is all that remains of the house. It lay next door to Ivy Villa on Upper Park Road on the corner of Denison Road and this coach house is off Denison Road. In 1977 it was converted into a two-bedroomed mews house with a walled garden.

Thornbury, known earlier as Hopeville, House on the corner of Upper Park Road on the right and Oxford Place. This now derelict shell housed various well-known people from the 1830s: George Hadfield, MP for Sheffield, Alderman William Romaine Callender, senior MP, Philip Kessler, merchant and William Hertz, merchant. In 1938 it was the Brookfield Hotel.

Gartness on Upper Park Road. This Gothic style, large, unusual house was designed by Joseph Crowther for a rich client but long stood derelict and dilapidated, a fate that has befallen several of the park's large houses. In the 1880s it was home to the East India merchant William Gaddum. After the First World War TocH used it for many years as a hostel for homeless men. It has just been demolished.

five

Churches
and Schools

A sketch of Birch Chapel-of-Ease, Birch-in-Rusholme. Erected as a family chapel in around 1596, it became an influential church for South Manchester and by 1636 was drawing its congregation from Birch, Slade, Rusholme, Grindlow, Chorlton, Rushford and Levenshulme. This brick chapel provided oak pews for 350 people. During the 1600s it was a centre for Dissenters (see pp. 104-5), but by 1844 it was too small for current demands and was demolished.

A drawing of the church of St James, Birch-in-Rusholme, in 1859. Architect M. Derick designed this church with its dignified, Gothic exterior, rose window and a south-west tower culminating in a tall spire. It cost £4,300 to build; Archdeacon George Anson gave £2,000 and public subscriptions provided the rest.

Above: St James's, Birch-in-Rusholme, Anglican church, off Danes Road, 1905. This 1846 replacement for old Birch chapel provided seven hundred seats (four hundred free in the centre and the rest paid on the sides). Gore Brook flows past the churchyard gate. The apparently rural setting was by virtue of its position between Birch Fields Park and the playing fields of Manchester Grammar school.

Right: St James's Anglican church, Birch. Bells first rang out on St James's Day on 25 July 1863. In 1907 the Anson chapel was added as a gift from Sir William Anson.

The lych-gate of St James's church, Birch, in 1902. The inscription over the gateway reads: 'The wages of sin is death. The sting of death is sin'. To the right of the gate lay old Birch chapel and the early gravestones. In 1850 a rectory was added, funded by selling some of the endowment fund land.

Birch parish rooms in the early 1900s. Erected in 1897 and enlarged in 1903 by the Revd Buller, they were built near the church on land given by Sir William Anson. Sales of Work and bazaars were held in what became a community centre for Birch.

Children outside the lych-gate of St James's church, Birch, in the 1940s. In 1979 the church was closed for worship and declared redundant in 1981. The congregation was united with the church of the Holy Innocents in Fallowfield. The church building was saved by conversion to a private house in 1982 and is now used as a home for young people.

Archdeacon George Henry Greville Anson, son of General Sir William Anson and a descendant of John Dickinson (see p. 55). His brother Sir John Anson was patron of Birch church, where George was minister for fifty-three years (1846-1890). Archdeacon of Manchester (1870-1890) and chaplain to bishops, he also helped to found Rusholme Local Board of Health and Rusholme public hall. On his death in 1898 he was buried near his church.

Above: Holy Trinity, Platt Anglican church off Platt Lane, viewed from Platt Fields, in 1913. Thomas Carill Worsley of Platt Hall commissioned Edmund Sharpe, for whom it was his second experimental, terracotta or 'pot' church, having terracotta inside and out, grooved to resemble chiselled stone. Costing £5,600, it seated 650. Thomas originally named it Trinity to contrast with Unitarian Platt chapel, which he once patronised (see p. 105). He won his competition to have Holy Trinity open before St James's church in 1846.

Left: Holy Trinity, Platt church, in 1907. The delicate, pink coloured, octagonal spire, 170ft high on its tower with flying buttresses, became warped and twisted as the terracotta cracked and it had to be rebuilt in 1912. The church itself had been restored twice. This rectory was added in 1888, a parish hall on Wilmslow Road in 1900 and a church hall east of the church in 1967.

Above: Platt day schools on Platt Lane in the late 1800s. The first day school in Rusholme was probably on Nelson Street by the Working Men's club in the 1840s. Platt day schools were sited in the east end of the barn-like outbuildings of Platt Hall in the early 1850s. In 1861 the school was replaced, by Platt schools of Holy Trinity church on Grove Street. William Royle attended both Platt day schools and was one of the first pupils at the new school.

Below: The building that housed Holy Trinity National day schools on the corner of Grove Street and Summer Place from 1861 and then as a state primary school until 1968. Holy Trinity then bought it as their Youth club house 'The Platters' and later it became the Holy Trinity House family centre for the Save the Children charity.

Above: Standard Five of St Agnes's Anglican church day schools on Clitheroe Road in the 1920s. The church of St Agnes, Birch-in-Rusholme on Hamilton Road, designed by the architect brothers James Medland and Henry Taylor, was consecrated in 1885. A rectory was added on St Agnes Road in 1928. The church, although united in 1997 with that of St John with St Cyprian in Longsight, still continues. The school was opened in 1885 and extended in 1890 and 1904.

Left: A blue plaque on Platt Unitarian chapel on Wilmslow Road. Birch Chapel of Ease was Anglican but in 1646 its minister John Wigan set up Congregationalism there and probably influenced Charles Worsley of Platt Hall. Robert Birch as minister there in 1662 was one of two thousand ministers ejected from his chapel as a Non-conformist. From 1672 Revd Henry Finch was allowed to hold Congregational services at Birch Hall, until George Birch dismissed him.

The earliest Platt chapel on Wilmslow Road. Revd Henry Finch, after leaving Birch chapel, preached in private houses licensed for Dissenting worship until 1699, when Ralph Worsley of Platt Hall gave land, called Blake Flatt, for a chapel. So Non-Conformity came to Rusholme in the form of Congregationalism, becoming Unitarianism by the early nineteenth century. An open belfry was added in 1718 and as the congregation outgrew the 128 sittings the chapel was demolished in 1790.

The second Platt chapel, which was built north of Nico Ditch in 1791 (see p. 66). A west chapel was dedicated for the Worsleys of Platt Hall but in 1830 the Worsleys left to build Holy Trinity church. In the 1880s the walls and roof were raised to add a gallery at the south end and the bell tower moved from north to south, together with the main door. In 1970 with falling numbers the chapel closed. Now Manchester Amateur Photographic Society owns the building.

Revd W.H. and Mrs Finney, in retirement outside Birkin church, Yorkshire, in the early 1900s. For twenty-five years rector of Platt chapel, he was well known for his care of the poor and his work with all churches. Both Platt and Birch chapels were led by strong ministers but with differing views. Revd John Wigan, a fervent Independent, resigned from Birch to join Cromwell's army. Revd Robert Birch led Congregational worship in Birch chapel and Revd Henry Finch held services in houses until Platt chapel was built.

Rusholme Congregational chapel on Wilmslow Road in the early 1900s. Congregationalism resumed at Kingthorpe Grove as a Sunday school off Moor Street from 1839. Next they moved to Holford's Row (now John Street) and then to a small, former Baptist chapel on Moor Street from 1853. This new chapel was opened in 1864, costing £7,260 and seating 650.

Rusholme Congregational chapel in the early 1900s. This Gothic, brick building, designed by Sir Alfred Waterhouse, had a tall tower and short spire. Its clock, framed by four steep gables, including a bell weighing eighteen hundredweight, was added in 1873 by public subscription. Manchester Corporation later maintained this illuminated, landmark clock on Wilmslow Road. The church was closed by 1969 and demolished in 1978.

Revd Thomas Campbell Finlayson of Glasgow for twenty-seven years minister at the Rusholme Congregational chapel. He was well loved in the area, a charming and learned pastor. He wrote books on religion, including a book of sermons. He married Helen Melland to Herbert Asquith. He died in 1893 aged only fifty-seven and was buried in his native Glasgow.

Dr Frederick Melland, 'grand old man of Rusholme', where he lived for over seventy years, working as a doctor until he was seventy. A keen politician, he helped to establish Rusholme public library and Rusholme Local Board of Health, as well as this Congregational chapel. He was a choir member and here in 1877 his daughter Helen married the future prime minister, barrister Herbert Asquith. Frederick died in 1911.

The Union Baptist chapel on Oxford Road (late Street), *c.* 1910. The Baptists after using small chapels on Moor and Oxford Streets (1840s-1860s), opened this larger chapel in 1869. Designed by brothers, James Medland and Henry Taylor, it cost £22,000 and seated around 1,300 people. Gothic in style, its west front, seen here, was richly ornate with moulded and ornamental brick and stone work and a large rose window.

Above: The interior of Union chapel in 1869. The south-east corner housed a lecture hall for about four hundred people. In the south-west corner the bell tower rose 120ft high, capped by a spire. Inside the church was galleried. There were also fourteen classrooms for Sunday school. The church was later closed and demolished.

Right: A sketch of a church parade in Whitworth Park with Union chapel in the background in 1889. The chapel lay directly opposite the park across Oxford Road and just within the border of Rusholme with Chorlton-on-Medlock. The great, circular-headed windows are clearly visible on the south side of the building.

Left: Revd Dr Alex McLaren from Scotland, the second pastor of the Baptists from 1858. He oversaw the building of Union chapel and extended the Baptists' work to Gorton and Hulme. He also acquired the People's Institute on Nelson Street for Baptist work and became its president.

Below: A sketch of the Baptist Theological college on Brighton Grove in 1889. This Gothic style building lay on the north side of the grove, appearing after the Brighton Grove scheme fell through (see pp. 34-5). In the 1920s this fine building was replaced by a second set of buildings, which in turn were partially replaced, under the guidance of the Revd H.L. Wata in 1962.

The chapel of the former Baptist College on Brighton Grove. This remains from the 1962 rebuild. In 1985 the Independents, the Baptists, Congregationalists and the Methodists, formed a partnership for Theological education and the college was renamed Luther King House.

The Wesleyan Methodist chapel on Dickenson Road. In 1826 a Sunday school was started in some cottages on Granny Lane (later Monmouth Street) by lay preacher Charles Beswick of Ardwick. A chapel followed in 1829, erected by Mr Fernley of Platt Hall. In 1862 this building replaced it on Dickenson Road but closed in around 1940. It was used as a film and later television studio (see pp. 118-120).

Left: Thomas Lowe, 'father of Wesleyan Methodism' in Rusholme. He lived here for fifty-six years until his death in 1892 aged seventy-eight. He helped to found the Working Men's club on Nelson Street and also Rusholme public hall and chaired the Jubilee celebrations in 1887. He loved astronomy and promoted temperance, whose first society in Rusholme he founded in 1845 at the chapel on Moor Street.

Below: A class at Manchester High School for Girls in 1956. Front first left sits Sandra Tomlinson (née Goodman). Manchester High School for Girls, founded in 1874 on Portland Place in the city, moved to Dover Street in around 1880. In 1936 the school paid £11,000 to purchase Grangethorpe House off Wilmslow Road in Rusholme from the Manchester Royal Infirmary.

The first eleven hockey team at Manchester High School for Girls in 1959. The team include Sandra Tomlinson (goal keeper), Heather Clark, Gillian Martin, Gillian Lowood, Jean Armour, Anne Barlow, Margaret Wood, Margaret Green, Jean Alcorn and Jennifer Taylor. There was a plan to demolish Grangethorpe, rebuild it and turn the old wards into classrooms but in 1940 a landmine destroyed the school. A new school was opened in 1951 (see pp. 30-32).

A girls' class outside Heald Place municipal day schools off Claremont Road in the 1920s. It opened in 1928 and by 1947 included senior boys', junior mixed and infants' departments, plus an evening institute and Civic youth centre. The entertainer Sevine, a ventriloquist with a doll called Daisy May, was educated here. The buildings were demolished, except for the red brick girls' school.

A class at Rusholme public hall day school on the corner of Wilmslow and Dickenson Roads in 1864. With the forty-two boys are head teacher James Royds and drawing master Mr Hadfield. The public hall was the centre of life for the town and included a public library. Back row, from left to right: George Warburton, Charlie Hobday, Tony Alton, Charlie Barton, -?-, Edwin Hyde, Billy Pettigrew, Harry Gould. Second row from back: Willie Wilde, Harry Royle, Bob Brunt, Jack Mawrey, Arthur Stringer, Tom Froggatt, Joe Mottram, Will Charlton, Edward Smith. Third row: George Barton, Will Palin, Tom Hobson, Marmaduke Whitty, George Palin, Will Whitty, Harry Nall, Tom Fothergill, John Charlton, John Mottershead, Tom Kellam, Ben Davis, Bob Nall, Billy Hawksby, Billy Howarth. Fourth Row: John Priestly, Will Priestly, Will Kellam, Billy Henson, Arthur Bond, Tom Charlton, Jimmy Royds, ? Stringer, Arthur Smith, Charlie Bond.

six

Entertainment and Leisure

May Day on Moor Street, in the early 1900s. In Rusholme's more rural days there were many traditional celebrations. The Wakes holidays were on the last Sunday of July and centred in Moor Street with stalls and roundabouts. The annual Rush Cart procession took place on St Oswald's Day on 5 August. The cart was made at Withington and travelled from Fallowfield to Rusholme. There was a band and Morris Dancers, who called at Platt Hall to receive refreshments from the Worsley family. The last Rush Cart procession was in 1882.

The programme cover for Leslie's Rusholme Pavilion on Wilmslow Road next to the Birch Villa Hotel. Harry Leslie, aged twenty-eight, left his job as a clerk to become a comic and ventriloquist. He set up his own theatre in 1904, first in a marquee and then in a permanent pavilion in around 1907. For almost forty years, he ran Pierrot and concert party shows, and had a series of his own companies, The Criterions and The Nobodies, and presented others, such as the Cabaret Kittens, the March Hares, the Brownies and the Quaintesques. The impresario Jack Hylton was also a touring performer here.

Above: The cast of the Rusholme repertory theatre on stage in their Christmas production *Katawampus* in 1924. The Rusholme theatre set up in the old horse tram depot (see p. 10) in 1911 as the Rusholme Electric theatre, which showed films and variety shows, boasting 'High-Class Cinematograph and Vaudeville'. From 1923 Mr Belt ran the Rusholme repertory theatre here, putting on hundreds of shows.

Right: Advertisement for the Rusholme theatre on the corner of Wilmslow Road and Great Western Street. Artists like Mary Hayley Bell, Wendy Hiller, Sir Donald Wolfit, Joan Littlewood and Robert Donat appeared here. Financial problems and lack of support forced closure in the 1930s. In the 1940s the theatre became a cinema and continued until closure in 1970. Asian films were screened later until fire damage brought final closure in 1982.

RUSHOLME THEATRE.

Corner of WILMSLOW RD., & GREAT WESTERN ST.,

All Palatine Road and Circular Route Cars stop at the doors.

Proprietors ... ... THE RUSHOLME THEATRE LTD.
Resident Manager .. .. .. Mr. HEMSWORTH LINLEY

HIGH-CLASS

Cinematograph & Vaudeville

(The Most Perfect Pictures ever Produced).

JULY 7th WEEK.

BROS. ST. JOHN
GAERTNER & MAY
SARA ROSEBURY

Our Pictures are the best in Manchester.

CHANGE OF PROGRAMME EVERY MONDAY AND THURSDAY.

6-50 - 8-45 TWO COMPLETE PERFORMANCES NIGHTLY. 9 -11

Admission 3d. and 6d.   Reserved Seats, 1/-.

Matinee, Saturday at 2-30 p.m.

Children, 2d. to all parts at Matinees.   Telephone, 692.

Rusholme Theatre — advert

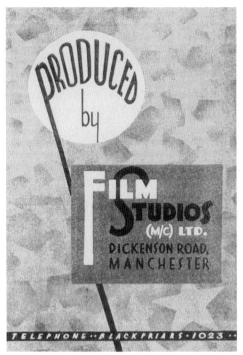

Left: The logo of the Film Studios (M/C) Ltd on Dickenson Road, just off Wilmslow Road. Set up by John Bleakeley in 1947 in the former Wesleyan Methodist church (see p. 111), it was the only feature film studio outside London at the time. It produced many money spinning Northern comedy films, employing music hall stars such as Sandy Powell, Norman Evans, Jimmy James, Frank Randle, Tessie O'Shea, Jimmy Clitheroe, Jimmy Jewell and George Formby.

Below: A photograph, signed 'for Bruce' by both Frank Randle and Tessie O'Shea, entitled 'That's My Man', showing them in the film *Somewhere in Politics*, filmed at the studios in 1948. Other films starring Frank Randle included *School for Randle* and *Holidays with Pay*.

"THAT'S MY MAN"

FILM STUDIOS (Manchester) LTD.

Above: Another photograph of Frank Randle and fellow actors at the film studios in *It's A Grand Life*, filmed in 1953. It was filmed partly in the grounds of Xaverian College in Victoria Park. 'Manchester's Hollywood' produced dozens of feature films, complete with Northern accents, which were box office hits. The advent of television finally led to the studio's decline, film-making became uneconomical and they closed down in 1954.

Right: The Roll of Honour for those who served in the First World War from Rusholme Conservative club. The names include those of members and their sons and also the MP Major P.K. Glazebrook. The Conservative club first operated on the east side of Wilmslow Road, between the Victoria Park entrance and Rusholme Grove in the early 1900s. By 1929 it was at Antwerp House on Kent Road West, where it continued.

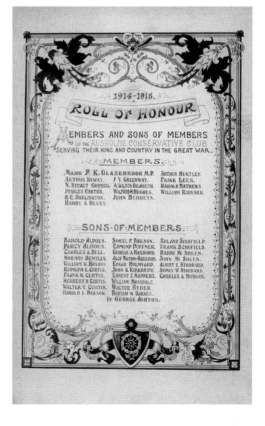

The old Wesleyan church building when used by the BBC in 1965. In 1956 this was the first regional television studio outside London, beating Granada by just a month. It was used on a drive-in basis with a mobile control room, as space was so restricted. Here the BBC Northern Light Orchestra rehearsed and performed live with their conductor Alyn Ainsworth. In 1957 *News from the North* became the region's news service, read at different times by Tom Naisby, Philip Dobson, Roger Moffat and Randal Herley, who travelled by taxi from Broadcasting House in London to Manchester. From here Jimmy Saville hosted *Top of the Pops* and Val Doonican and Simon Dee broadcast. The studio closed in 1973.

The plaque on the side wall of the People's Institute commemorating the renaming of the hall the 'McLaren Memorial Hall' in 1910 after Revd Dr McLaren. There are also initialised bricks as part of the foundation wall. In the 1890s the Baptists of Union chapel took over the chapel and their pastor Revd McLaren became its superintendent. In 1910 they virtually rebuilt it in memory of him. The hall finally closed in 1964.

The People's Institute on the corner of Eileen Grove and Victory (late Nelson) Street off Platt Lane. It was built in 1872, the entire cost being met by James Ryder. Mrs Langworthy later had more rooms added. One of the earliest boys' clubs in Manchester met here. It now belongs to the Shahjalal Mosque as an Islamic centre.

Above: At an annual talent competition on the bandstand in Platt Fields park. Jack Hynes took this photograph of his son Robert, who was playing the banjo.

Left: Jack Hynes, the 'Wizard of the Banjo', rehearsing for the BBC Musical Variety radio show regional programme on 16 February 1932. Jack and his family lived on Dorset Avenue in Rusholme and he was in demand for his banjo playing and entertained the troops in ENSA shows during the war.

Robert Hynes, with his banjo, being presented with the first prize in a talent contest by Joan Edwards (third from left) in 1957. The Manchester-based Henry's store held this talent contest. Joan Edwards was a well-known American vocalist in the 1940s and 50s with her own radio programme and show.

The group known as Pete Maclaine and the Clan on their formation in 1963. From the left, at the front, are Pete Bocking, Pete Maclaine and Brian Day with John Hynes of Rusholme behind them. This Manchester group performed all over the country including a show in London with the Rolling Stones.

PETE MACLAINE AND THE CLAN

A football team from Rusholme in the 1930s. In 1934/5 the Rusholme Amateur football league was founded by L.E. (Eddie) Walker, who was its secretary and organiser. Leslie Lever MP was president and there were numerous trophies to be won. By the Second World War there were seven divisions with one hundred and eight clubs from all over Manchester and Salford. That involved arranging fifty-four games each Saturday. After the war, however, the Sunday League took over in popularity.

The tennis courts, originally eight in number, in Birch Fields Park in 1905. They were separated from the main park by the Favourite Walk and Birch Brook. In the distance is the outline of the tall house nicknamed the Pepperpot, because of its shape.

By the lake in Whitworth park, *c.* 1910. The Union Baptist chapel lies in the background.

On the lake at Platt Fields in the early 1900s. Across the water is the boathouse for the launches and rowing boats.

Above: The council of the Anson golf club sitting outside their clubhouse in 1903. This clubhouse with its verandah was opened, together with the golf course, in 1893. The course lay over about fifty acres off Birch Hall Lane near Victoria Park. It was founded by Sir William Anson Bart MP, who was also its president and presented the Anson cup to the winner of the annual competition.

Left: The Anson golf club trophy. It was presented to Anson golf club by John Croall of Edinburgh, whose brother was a member of the Royal and Ancient golf club at St Andrew's. The trophy has one engraving: it was won by G. Jennison in 1902. The club closed in around 1920 and the course was built over for the Anson housing estate.

Brothers Robert and John Hynes aged about eight and fourteen, respectively, dressed in Boys' Brigade uniforms, standing in their back yard in 1954. Their father Jack snapped them at home at 26 Dorset Avenue with an old curtain draped over the back wall as a backdrop. They belonged to the 59th Manchester Brigade at Platt Lane Methodist church.

A comic postcard of the 1920s. This was a stock picture to which was added the name of the town. It seems a far cry from the leafy, (inland) residential suburb that was Rusholme.

Other local titles published by Tempus

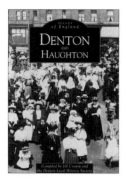

Denton and Haughton

JILL CRONIN AND DENTON LOCAL HISTORY SOCIETY

The neighbouring townships of Denton and Haughton were both famous for hat making but mining, farming and the cotton industry were also important employers in past times. This splendid collection of over 200 old photographs borrowed from local people provides a delightful insight into those times, showing people at work and play through the decades of the twentieth century.

0 7524 0757 0

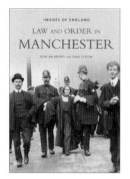

Law and Order in Manchester

DUNCAN BROADY

This fascinating collection of over 200 old photographs was compiled from the extensive photoarchives at the Greater Manchester Police Museum. Along with detailed captions they provide a valuable account of the history of the Greater Manchester Police Force and its changing role in the social history of the city, including descriptions of wartime Manchester, the arrest of Suffragettes, events, occasions and examples of detective work. This book is sure to appeal to anyone who has lived in Manchester, either on the right or the wrong side of the law!

0 7524 3713 5

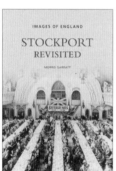

Stockport Revisited

MORRIS GARRATT

This is the second selection of old photographs of Stockport in the series and it includes scenes from around the whole of the enlarged Metropolitan area. The book contains important archive material including images of Christy's hat works, the building of the town hall, the Staircase café, the Blue Lagoon swimming pool and the day St John's church school caught fire.

0 7524 4172 8

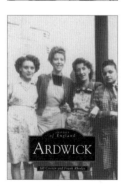

Ardwick

JILL CRONIN AND FRANK RHODES

Ardwick was one of Manchester's first suburbs and this collection of over 200 old photographs illustrates life and times in the area over a period of one hundred years. In the nineteenth century the area had parks and gardens and was a desirable residential quarter for the rich and successful. Later its character changed as it attracted industry and the cramped housing associated with it. As the area changes once again, with building clearances and new developments, this book provides a timely record of what went before.

0 7524 2473 4

If you are interested in purchasing other books published by Tempus, or in case you have difficulty finding any Tempus books in your local bookshop, you can also place orders directly through our website

www.tempus-publishing.com